First published 1979
Macdonald Educational
Holywell House
Worship Street
London EC2A 2EN

© Macdonald Educational
Limited, 1979

ISBN 0 356 06304 6
  (cased edition)
ISBN 0 356 06509 X
  (limp edition)

Made and printed by
New Interlitho
Milan
Italy

**Editor**
Julia Kirk

**Assistant Editor**
John Liebmann

**Design**
Sarah Tyzack

**Production**
Rosemary Bishop

**Picture Research**
Jan Croot

**Illustrators**
Jeffrey Anderson/
  B. L. Kearley
Jon Blake
Jeff Burn/Temple Art
Bryan Evans/Temple Art
Pamela Goodchild/
  B. L. Kearley
Donald Harley/
  B. L. Kearley
Hayward Art Group
Peter Morgan/John Martin
  & Artists
Edward Osmond/
  B. L. Kearley
Michael Whittlesea/
  Temple Art

Macdonald Educational

# The Saxons

**Tony D. Triggs**

# The Saxons

In the fifth century AD many of the people who lived in what is now Denmark, North Germany and North Holland left their home and rowed westwards. These were the Saxons, whose name probably comes from the short sword, or *seax*, which they used.

Like their neighbours, the Angles, Jutes and Frisians, the Saxons arrived in Britain as invaders. After they had overcome the native Britons they settled as farmers.

For most of the 600 years of the Saxon period, England was made up of separate kingdoms. The first of these to become rich and powerful was the kingdom of Kent. Its magnificent jewellery shows that it must have been very prosperous.

The next great kingdom was East Anglia. The royal graveyard at Sutton Hoo, in Suffolk, has revealed the treasure which was buried with the kings.

The third great kingdom was Northumbria, formed by the merging of Deira and Bernicia. In its heyday, Northumbria was a land of monasteries. The monks produced books by hand which often included pages of delicate and beautiful colouring.

The king of Mercia in its most prosperous period was the mighty Offa. Apart from the great earthworks of Offa's Dyke, the epic poem *Beowulf* remains as a legacy of Mercia's greatest days. The story tells of monsters and of the hero who fought them.

The Saxons' real-life hero was King Alfred, who led the kingdom of Wessex to power.

This book will tell you about the coming of the Saxons to Britain, their society, their myths, their crafts, and their way of life.

# Contents

# Wolves from the sea

In the third and fourth centuries AD Roman Britain was under attack. Some of the fiercest attackers came from the sea. They landed on undefended beaches and plundered the nearest homestead. Then they made a quick getaway.

The Romans built signal stations and fortresses on coasts where attacks were frequent. But by the start of the fifth century Rome itself was in danger. The Romans withdrew from far-off places like Britain. They left the native Britons to defend the land.

The Britons' worst enemies were the Picts, who came from Scotland. Although Saxons had also been attacking Britain, King Vortigern invited the Saxon chieftains

Saxon warriors raided only for plunder at first. Later they began an all-out conquest of the native Britons.

Hengest and Horsa to bring soldiers to defend the country. In return they received land which they were allowed to farm, and where they settled.

In the middle of the fifth century they sent for reinforcements. Before long, Hengest and Horsa turned against the Britons and fought them. Horsa was killed, but Hengest founded the kingdom of Kent.

There were battles for over fifty years as more and more Saxon warriors came to Britain, determined to settle. The Britons resisted, but by about the year 530 most of England belonged to the Saxons. The Britons died in battle, fled westwards, or were enslaved.

# Who were the Saxons?

The true Saxons came from northern Germany. When we speak of the Saxons we often include their neighbours the Angles, Jutes and Frisians.

Many of these Saxons lived on islands surrounded by marsh or sea. Their land was often very poor and thin, and they did not have enough of it. The only way they could get more was by going abroad and settling other people's land. This was why they conquered the Britons.

The Saxons crossed to Britain in rowing-boats. Some were large enough for forty warriors. To reach Britain they rowed across the North Sea, which can often be very stormy. Many crews must have gone to the bottom.

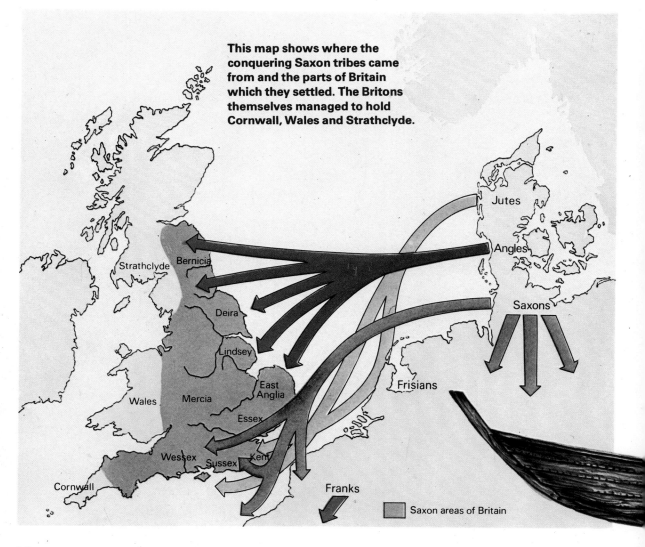

This map shows where the conquering Saxon tribes came from and the parts of Britain which they settled. The Britons themselves managed to hold Cornwall, Wales and Strathclyde.

Jutes

Angles

Saxons

Frisians

Franks

Strathclyde

Bernicia

Deira

Lindsey

Wales

Mercia

East Anglia

Essex

Wessex

Sussex

Kent

Cornwall

Saxon areas of Britain

◀ Before they came to Britain many Saxons had to try to farm on very poor soil.

▼ Parents often passed land to their eldest son. The others had to find land for themselves.

The invaders found that rivers were an ideal way of getting deep into enemy country. The boats were narrow and easy to handle. They were light enough to be carried by the crew if necessary.

The Romans had left some fine roads behind, but there were very few of them. Elsewhere travel on land was difficult. Hills, forests, bogs and broad rivers blocked the way.

The Saxons were used to such natural barriers. Each boatload formed their own little settlement, and the settlements grouped themselves under local leaders. Saxon England at first was a patchwork of little kingdoms, each with its tribal chieftain or king. As time went on, some of the kingdoms took over their neighbours. This was often by military conquest, and so the kingdoms became fewer but stronger. The Saxons acknowledged one of the kings as overlord. He was known as the Bretwalda.

▼ The Saxon lands in Europe became overcrowded.

▲ Large areas of the Saxon homelands consisted of sand-dunes or bogs, and were no use for farming. The Frisians made artificial islands, but these quickly became overcrowded.

▼ The Saxons rowed their boats, though they knew about sails. The boats were made from planks joined by rivets, and carried forty men. They sat in pairs, each man with an oar.

# Freeman and slave

A thane and his wife. They were rich enough to have fine clothes and horses.

A churl was a freeman but he had to work hard at ploughing and other farming jobs.

This man is a slave. He had to do the hardest and most unpleasant jobs on his master's land.

Beneath the king, the main ranks of Saxon society were 'freeman' and 'slave'. Freemen owned land and money, and many of them owned slaves. If a freeman was working for another man he could leave to seek a new employer. The law protected freemen's rights, but also gave them certain duties such as military service.

Slaves owned hardly anything. They were someone else's property, and could never leave their owner unless he chose to sell them or free them. The law gave slaves very little protection, and their owners often treated them harshly.

There were two ranks of freemen. The richer ones were known as 'thanes' and the poorer ones were known as 'churls'. To qualify as a thane a man had to own at least five

▲ The thane is receiving a young boy into slavery. His family are churls, and they are selling him because they are very poor. Slavery was also a punishment for crime, and prisoners of war were sometimes made to work as slaves for their captors.

hides of land. One hide was enough land to grow food for one family. With so much land, a thane did not do much of the farming himself. The harder jobs, like mucking out the cattle, were done by his slaves.

A thane often had craftsmen, such as a blacksmith, attached to his household. The craftsmen were churls. They were freemen, not slaves. These did not usually have any land of their own, but were provided for by the thane.

Other churls usually owned just one hide of land. The law allowed all freemen to keep slaves, but with so little land these churls could only produce enough food to feed their own families. They were often very poor, and were sometimes no better off than slaves.

# The King and the law

▶ The king and queen receiving pleas for mercy. Someone who had been caught stealing might beg not to be enslaved.

◀ The Witan discussed new laws with the king. The Saxon word 'Witan' meant 'wise men'.

The most powerful man in a Saxon kingdom was the king, but he did not rule alone. To assist him he had a group of wise advisers called the Witan. The Witan members were among the highest-ranking thanes of the kingdom.

Many of the laws were designed to discourage the habit of killing in vengeance. If someone was murdered, the victim's family felt it their duty to kill the murderer. Under the laws, the family received money from the murderer instead. The payment was known as a *wergild*, meaning man-price. The amount to be paid depended on the social rank of the murdered man. A thane's *wergild* was 1,200 shillings, but a churl's was only 200 shillings.

A freeman who could not afford a *wergild* or fine was put into slavery. Slaves never had much money and so it was no use asking a slave to pay a *wergild*. Slaves who did wrong were flogged, hanged or put in the stocks.

The law was administered by 'ealdormen', who each took charge of a large part of the kingdom. Ealdormen had sheriffs to help them. Sheriffs supervised public meetings, witnessed transactions, and tried to stop traders from cheating. The sheriff saw that coins were made to the proper standard and that cattle-rustlers were dealt with. In time of war he called men to arms.

▲ The king is receiving an oath of allegiance. The man, who may have come from a foreign country, is promising that he will be a true and loyal subject.

▶ The king supervised the testing of gold. A certain weight of gold was put into a butt of water. If the gold was pure the water rose just to the brim but did not overflow. If the water overflowed, the king knew that a cheap metal had been mixed with the gold.

**Saxon coins**

If one man wounded another in a fight, a feud might begin between them. This could become just as serious as a feud between families after a murder. Saxon law laid down the amounts to be paid in compensation for injuries, just as it laid down the *wergild* as compensation for murder. A man who had his nose cut off could claim 60 shillings from the person who did it. A big toe was worth 20 shillings, and a little toe was worth nine. The payment was often made in front of other people. They saw to it that justice was done according to the law, and the dispute was settled.

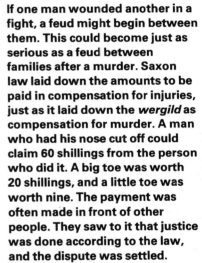

# Jewellery for rich and poor

The Saxons made an amazing variety of jewellery. It included buckles, necklaces, shoulder-clasps and rings. Rich people used to fasten their cloaks with circular brooches of gold or silver. The poorer people had cross-shaped brooches, which were often made of bronze.

Jewellery for the king was specially made, with each piece to a different design. With cheaper ornaments there were sometimes many pieces made to the same pattern.

Even for his best work in gold and garnets a Saxon jeweller used well-established methods. First he made a base-plate of solid gold. He brazed or soldered gold wires to the base-plate to make a pattern of shallow holes. Into each hole he fitted a piece of gold foil, and then a tiny piece of garnet.

Garnet is a semi-precious stone. Like any stone it is difficult to cut, yet the Saxon jewellers cut garnet to shape even down to the size of a pin-head. The gold foil had a roughened surface which reflected light. This made each tiny stone sparkle brilliantly when light shone upon it.

The Saxons liked decorations based on animals. They often made the animals' bodies, limbs, and jaws or beaks extremely long. They tangled the animals up to make a pattern called animal interlace.

▲ Necklaces, brooches and pins. The pins probably decorated a woman's hair. The patterned glass pendant on the necklace at the top was made by melting coloured glass rods. The other pendants are coins.

◄ Poor villagers bought jewellery from travelling pedlars.

► This solid gold buckle belonged to a king. It is decorated with animal interlace.

◄ This is one of the royal shoulder-clasps which were found at Sutton Hoo in Suffolk. It is made entirely of gold, except for the garnets and bluish glass which decorate the surface. The halves come apart if the central pin is removed. The two halves were sewn to the garment, which was fastened by inserting the pin.

► This close-up of part of a circular brooch shows the fine workmanship. Some of the garnets have fallen out, revealing the speckled gold foil which the jeweller placed behind each stone to make it glisten.

# The Saxon village

The Saxon village was full of activity. The buildings were made of wood, and they had to be replaced when they rotted away. Often the walls were made of pliable sticks, called wattles. They were woven together and then daubed with mud to keep out draughts. Some of the huts in the village were workshops for industries such as weaving.

The Roman historian Tacitus wrote about the Saxon peoples. He said that none of them lived in cities. They made no use of stone or tiles. They could not even bear to see houses built in rows. Centuries later the Saxons referred to cities left behind by the Romans as *enta geweorc*, which was Saxon for 'giants' buildings'. The Saxons left them to crumble.

The Saxons were highly skilled wood-workers and built all their houses of timber. Although none have survived to the present day, we can find out about them from clues buried in the soil, where their villages once stood. After carefully removing the top-most layers of soil, the dark stains left behind by rotted posts and timbers can be seen. Archaeologists can trace the outlines of the buildings from the positions of these marks.

A Saxon village in England had groups of single-roomed buildings for sleeping, workshops and store houses. Each group was centred round a 'hall' or meeting house, probably one for each family.

The smaller houses were made with a framework of upright posts and horizontal beams covered with vertical planks for the walls, and neatly thatched with straw or reeds. Inside there was a wooden floor with an air-space or pit underneath which could be used for storage. These single-roomed houses were five or six metres long.

The halls did not have pits but were much larger, with a hearth in the middle. The whole family met and lived in their hall: uncles and aunts, brothers, sisters and slaves.

▼ In a low hut like this one the pit gave extra headroom. Taller huts had plenty of headroom anyway, so the pit could be boarded over. A clay hearth was built on the floor. A blazing fire was needed in winter, but must have been a cause of danger. Sometimes a hut was burned to the ground.

▶ At West Stow in Suffolk archaeologists are reconstructing a Saxon village. Groups of smaller huts surround family 'halls'. The house with the roof coming right down to the ground is how people used to think the houses there were built.

# Spring and summer

The Saxons came to England for better soil, but with simple tools it was still a hard job to get it ready for sowing. The sower is scattering wheat or barley.

Most Saxons worked on the land. Each village was really a farming community.

Cereal crops were most important. Oats and rye were grown, as well as wheat and barley. Cereals could be sown in the autumn, but the main time for sowing was the spring. Peas, beans and lentils were also sown in the spring.

Not all the crops were grown for food. Flax was grown for its fibres, which were woven into fine linen cloth. Woad and madder were grown for the colourful dyes they gave.

The Saxon villagers kept cattle, sheep, pigs and poultry. Most animals had special winter quarters, but at other times of year they were kept in the open. The pigs were

These people are using sickles to cut the wheat. They carted it away to be threshed, winnowed, and ground. Farm animals grazed on the stubble.

allowed to roam in the forests and fend for themselves. The cattle, sheep and poultry were allowed into fields by day . At night they were kept in small enclosures for protection. Someone watched over them all the time to save them from foxes and wolves. The Saxons used dogs to help in guarding and herding other animals.

Poultry were kept for their eggs and their meat. Cattle and sheep were kept for their milk, flesh and bone. The skin of the cattle provided leather, and this was turned into useful items such as belts and bottles. The sheep provided wool to be spun and woven into cloth. Both spinning and weaving were everyday activities in Saxon households.

The Saxons destroyed large areas of woodland to make new fields. They were still glad to have some woodland nearby. They needed wood for building and fencing.

These people are cutting hay with scythes. The hay was important in winter as food for the livestock. It was cut in the summer and carefully stored.

# Autumn and winter

These men are burning rotten stakes. Perhaps they had been used for several years for fences, pens and enclosures.

Pruning was an important task. Dead wood was cut away so that trees and bushes grew more strongly.

Ploughing was one of the main activities in autumn and winter. The plough was drawn by two or more oxen. The villagers shared their oxen to make up the team. Each family owned separate strips of land, but the work of ploughing was probably shared. They left a path of unploughed soil between each strip.

Each year one field in every two or three was left unploughed. Animals were kept in these fallow fields. The animals' manure kept the fields fertile.

Most villages had permanent meadowland and woodland nearby. In late summer and early autumn the meadows were mowed with scythes to make hay for winter fodder.

The men with flails are threshing the newly cut grain-crop to separate the grain from the straw.

The woodland provided building material and firewood. In the autumn the trees produced nuts to eat, and acorns to feed wild boar and the villagers' pigs.

During the autumn the villagers were busy with the grain, which was harvested at the end of the summer. The sheaves were beaten to separate the grain from the straw. The grain was then tossed in a breeze which blew away the pieces of chaff. This job was called 'winnowing'.

After it had dried thoroughly, the grain was ground. This was usually done with a quern, which consisted of a pair of heavy stone discs. The upper stone was turned by hand on the lower one, and the grain was ground between them.

Autumn was the season for slaughtering livestock.

A churl guides the plough. The man who is goading the oxen might have been a slave. The other man is sowing wheat or barley.

23

# Wool and weaving

The Saxons wove both wool and flax, but wool was the more important. Sheep-shearing was probably done by the men. The women washed and combed the wool. Then they spun it into yarn and wove it into cloth.

As well as making cloth for themselves the Saxons traded cloth abroad. It was probably their most important export. We know of this trade from a complaint by King Charlemagne of the Franks to King Offa of Mercia in AD 796. He complained that the Saxon merchants were selling his people cloaks that were too short.

▼ The shepherd's job was very important. Each morning he had to drive his sheep to pasture from their night-time enclosure. He then spent the day watching over them with his dogs to protect them from wolves. He also had to repair their pens.

The weaving looms were upright frames. The weighted threads of wool which hung down from the top are called the warp. Alternate threads of the warp were attached to a wooden bar called the heddle. The heddle had two positions. By moving it towards her the woman pulled forward the threads attached to it, so that they were in front of the others. She then passed her cross-thread from one side to the other between the two sets of warp threads. Next, she moved the heddle away from her. This allowed the threads attached to it to move to the rear of the others. Now she passed the cross-thread back in the space between them. She repeated these actions again and again, pushing the cross-threads upwards to add to the cloth she had already made.

◀ A wide range of products came from sheep and other farm animals. Some of the milk they gave was drunk. The rest was turned into butter and cheese. The animals supplied meat to eat and fat for the lamps. Their bone was used for making combs, and their horns made drinking cups.

▼ The seated woman is spinning. She is turning fleece into yarn by drawing it into a thread with her fingers. She has a weighted stick called a spindle which she spins so that it twists the yarn. This gives it extra strength.

▲ Shears, loom-weights, embroidery workbox and needles. Loom-weights were rings of baked clay which were tied to the warp threads on the loom to keep them taut.

# The smith and the potter

In Alfric's playlet someone says to the blacksmith, 'What do you give us but sparkling iron, thunderous beating and the puffing of bellows?' The blacksmith answers, 'Why do you speak like that when you can't even make a hole without my help? Where does the fisherman get his hook, or the cobbler his awl, or the tailor his needle?' He also made cauldrons, chains and shears.

**This potter has rolled out her lump of clay like a snake, then coiled it into the form of a pot. Another method was simply to shape the mass of clay.**

**To complete her pot the potter has to smooth it both inside and out. This makes the thickness even and gets rid of the coiled appearance.**

▲ This man is in charge of the kiln in which the pots are baked hard. He is making the fire burn more intensely by using bellows. This ensures that his finished pots will be reddish-brown. If the air supply is barely enough the pots turn out black. Sometimes the Saxons wanted them black, and purposely cut down the air supply.

Saxon pottery was both useful and decorative. Before they became Christian, the Saxons often burned their dead and buried the ashes in pottery funeral urns. Archaeologists have found some of the finest examples of Saxon pottery in cemeteries.

Funeral urns were often decorated. Some of them had patterns which were pressed into the wet clay by specially shaped pieces of antler. Pottery with the same design has been found in several different cemeteries. This shows that there was trade in pottery between districts.

Most Saxon potters shaped the clay by hand. When a batch of pots had dried, the potter baked them in an oven to make them really hard and strong. The simplest sort of oven was just a circular mud wall with a bonfire inside and a pile of pots in the middle. The potter kept the fire burning slowly by heaping it over with peat and an outer layer of soil.

Kilns gave better results. Saxon potters made their kilns with wattle and daub. They were dome-shaped with a chimney-hole at the top. Before completing the dome the potter stacked his pots inside. There was a hole at the base of the dome where the fire was burned. When the pots were ready the potter let the fire go out. He broke open the kiln and removed the pots. When he had another batch of pots he put them inside, repaired the kiln and lit another fire.

▼ Larger pots and urns were often decorated. Accidental markings on pots can also be of interest. Seeds baked into the surface can tell us what the Saxons ate.

# The fowler . . .

A Saxon monk called Alfric wrote a playlet in which a fowler, a hunter, and other workers are questioned about their ways of life. Let us see what the fowler can tell us:

*Tell us, fowler, how do you go about catching birds?*

I catch birds in many ways – with nets, with snares, with lime, by whistling, sometimes with a hawk and sometimes with traps.

*Can you tame hawks?*

Yes I can. What use would they be to me if I didn't know how to tame them?

*How do you feed your hawks?*

They feed themselves and me as well in winter, and in spring I let them fly away to the woods. I catch young hawks in the autumn and tame them. On their legs I put fetters, called jesses. Then I can keep them on a leash while they learn to bring me the birds they catch.

# . . . and the hunter

Now let us see what the hunter has to tell us:

*Hunter, how do you do your hunting?*

I weave myself nets and lay them in a likely place. I set my dogs chasing after the wild animals until they come to the nets unawares, so that they get snared. I kill them in the nets.

*Surely you can hunt without nets?*

Yes, I can catch the wild animals with swift dogs.

*Which animals do you catch most often?*

I catch stags and bears, roe deer and does, and sometimes hares. I was hunting yesterday.

*What did you catch?*

Two stags and a boar. I caught the stags in nets and I slew the boar. The dogs drove it towards me and I stabbed it to death.

*You must have been very brave. What do you do with what you've caught?*

I give the king whatever I catch because I am his huntsman.

*What does he give you?*

He clothes me well and feeds me. Sometimes he gives me a horse or a gold bracelet, so I willingly give my skill in return.

# Pastimes and sports

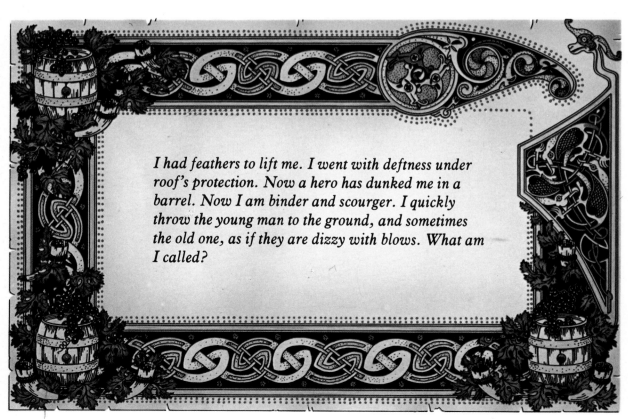

*I had feathers to lift me. I went with deftness under roof's protection. Now a hero has dunked me in a barrel. Now I am binder and scourger. I quickly throw the young man to the ground, and sometimes the old one, as if they are dizzy with blows. What am I called?*

▼ Villages sometimes had visits from travelling entertainers.

Heavy drinking was a favourite pastime among the Saxons. There were sometimes drinking parties over the bodies of dead people waiting for burial. Feasting was popular too. Often there was music and song at the feasts. The usual instrument played at feasts was the hand-harp or lyre. The Saxons also had several other sorts of musical instruments, including the bagpipes.

There were minstrels who played and sang, or the lyre could be passed from person to person with everyone taking a turn. As well as being good musicians, the Saxons enjoyed dancing too. Animal and juggling acts were probably taken from village to village by travelling entertainers. There was bull-baiting and bear-baiting.

The richer Saxons rode horses on hunting expeditions and in races. Saxon place-names help to confirm this. The name Hesketh means 'racecourse'. There were also special sites for athletic events. These have given us place-names like Plaistow, meaning 'games-field'.

The Saxons played a board-game called tafl. They made the pieces from animal bone and horses' teeth. The children probably used sheep's ankle bones as jacks or five-stones.

▶ This woman and her husband are playing a board-game called tafl. Tafl was played on a checkered board. One player tried to get a piece from the centre square to the edge of the board, but the other player had several pieces with which to attack it. The Saxons made their boards of wood. These have not survived, but playing-pieces and dice made of bone are often found in Saxon graves.

◀ The Saxons enjoyed making up elaborate riddles to ask each other. The answer to this one is 'mead', which is a drink made from honey. The 'feathers' in the riddle are the bees' wings which carried it to the hive. Now it is in a barrel as part of the mead. The mead makes people drunk, just as the riddle says.

# Food and drink

Animals grew fat in the summer. They were slaughtered in the autumn and the meat was salted to preserve it for the winter.

For food and drink the Saxons depended on what they could grow. They had to do without fruit from abroad, such as oranges and bananas. Some very small quantities of spices and grapes were imported, but these were only for the richest people.

Place-names show what the Saxons grew. It is easy to guess what fruits were grown at Appleton and Plumstead. Pears were grown at Parbold, and beans were grown at Banham. Peas were grown at Peasenhall. Most places grew a mixture of crops. Even in places named after a special crop, other crops were grown as well.

Grain crops were very important. Barley was used in the brewing of ale, and to make flour for baking. Wheat was also ground to make flour. Poor people mixed various grains to make soup or gruel. They did not often have any special meat like venison. Such meat was only eaten by people who were rich enough to have time to hunt, or rich enough to employ a hunter.

There is cream in the tub and one of the women is beating it to turn it into butter. The other woman is using a pair of wooden tools to shape the butter into pats.

Saxons obtained hardly any of their food from abroad but enjoyed a wide variety of local food. This included nuts and berries that grew in the wild, and various game.

► Bee-keeping was probably an occupation for experts, just as it is today.

▼ Swine that were kept for the following year were driven into the forest to fend for themselves on acorns and beech-mast.

Bee-keeping was an important occupation for the Saxons. Mead was their favourite alcoholic drink and they made it with fermented honey. They also used honey for sweetening food. They did not have any other form of sugar.

Salt was important too. The Saxons obtained it by evaporating sea-water or water from salty springs inland. They put the salt water in metal pans and burned wood underneath them. When all the water had boiled away the salt was left in the pan as a dry deposit. The Saxons relied on salt to preserve their meat and fish for the winter. They also used it in butter and cheese.

Alfric wrote about a fisherman who worked from a rowing-boat. He had several different ways of catching the fish. He had traps made of basket-work called creels. He also had nets and baited hooks. He caught eels, pike and trout from the rivers. From the sea he caught herring, plaice and sturgeon. As well as fish he caught lobsters, crabs and shellfish. Most of what he caught he took to the market to sell.

There were weirs across the rivers where the fast-flowing water carried the fish into special traps. People who fished on river banks had to give a share of the catch to the owner of the land.

33

# Meadhall and the heroic code

A king could call on any of the freemen he ruled to interrupt their farming and form an army. After the battle the men returned home. The king also had a bodyguard of soldiers who lived in the royal household.

The story of Lilla shows what a bodyguard might have to do. A stranger called Eumer had come to King Edwin's palace pretending to be a messenger. From the folds of his cloak he produced, not a scroll, but a dagger. As he lunged at King Edwin, Lilla threw himself in the way. The King survived but Lilla was killed.

In return for their devoted service a king treated his bodyguard well. They feasted with the king in his banqueting hall. The minstrel played his lyre and sang of great battles. There was so much drinking of mead that the banqueting halls were often called meadhalls. The king often gave out treasures of gold to his guests. A blazing fire kept everyone warm and roasted whatever the hunter had killed.

On the battlefield the bodyguard set all the other soldiers a good example. They fought with skill and they would fight to the death. Even if they saw the king killed they would carry on fighting his battle. This bond between retainer, or bodyguard, and king is sometimes known as the Saxons' Heroic Code.

▲ Drinking-glasses imitated the shape of the animals' horns which were also used. Later the glassmakers learned that a straighter shape was better, and made ornate claw-beakers. The drink even filled the bulges and loops that make up the claws.

▶ The meadhall was a place of feasting. The warriors hung their decorated shields around the walls. A slave served them with mead, and the minstrel sang songs of great battles.

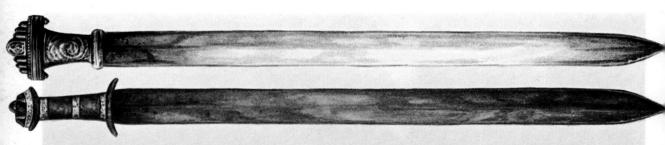

▲ Saxon kings often gave swords to their retainers. The Saxons prized fine swords. They passed them from father to son, and even gave them names.

▶ In 991, as Viking attackers overcame a Saxon force in the Battle of Maldon, a Saxon bodyguard described what loyalty meant to a retainer.

*Mind shall be mightier, manhood more mettlesome,*
*Spirit stronger even as lifeblood streams away.*
*Here lies our leader, slashed by axes,*
*The good one cut to the ground. Let him regret it forever*
*Who thinks to flee from this field of battle.*
*Though old in years, I'll not desert*
*So beloved a man: I shall lay down my life*
*In battle beside the body of my lord.*

# The story of Beowulf

Hrothgar, king of the Danes, built a mighty banqueting hall called Heorot. The monster Grendel heard the noise of feasting. At Heorot he found the retainers drunk and asleep. He devoured no less than thirty of them. Time after time Hrothgar's warriors were slaughtered.

Beowulf heard about Grendel and journeyed by sea and horseback to Heorot. He kept watch in the hall while other soldiers slept. Without warning Grendel burst through the door. He snatched a warrior from his couch to begin his feast. Greedy for more he grabbed at Beowulf. The benches were overturned as they fought ferociously. Suddenly there was a terrible howl as Beowulf tore Grendel's arm from his body. The soldiers hung the arm from a beam, and Grendel escaped to die.

Beowulf brandished Hrunting and whirled it round his head. He brought it savagely against the monster's neck, but it glanced away. Seizing her chance, the monster came at Beowulf with a fearsome knife. As he advanced he grasped a mighty sword which was standing against the rocky wall. Wielding it like an axe he cut off her head. He had saved Hrothgar's people again.

Beowulf returned to his homeland in southern Sweden. He became king and ruled in peace.

After many years the peace was broken when a runaway slave took refuge in a burial mound where a dragon lived. Inside the mound was a hoard of treasure, and when the slave left he took a jewelled goblet. The dragon was furious, and flew over the kingdom at night spewing fire at crops and houses.

*Beowulf* is the Saxons' greatest poem and one of the longest poems ever written. It must have been one of the favourites for recitation at feasts. Though written down in England it is full of memories of the Saxons' life in their old European home. The hero is a prince from southern Sweden. His name was Beowulf.

But the following night Grendel's mother came to Heorot to avenge her son. She snatched Aschere, Hrothgar's beloved adviser, and escaped to her home in a haunted lake.

At daybreak Beowulf set out with a troop of soldiers. They followed her tracks deep into lands where demons dwell. On a foreland above a bloodstained lake was Aschere's head.

Beowulf prepared for battle. Someone lent him Hrunting, an ancient sword which had never been known to fail. With Hrunting in his hand Beowulf dived into the lake. As the murky water swallowed him up he felt horns of strange creatures tearing at him savagely. Soon he found himself in a dry cave. There before him was the monster he was seeking, the mother of Grendel.

King Beowulf chose a dozen comrades to go with him to put an end to the dragon. As they neared his lair he ordered them to stand back so that he could fight the dragon alone. But Beowulf was soon in trouble. His shield gave him little protection from the dragon's flames, and his sword glanced off the dragon's scaly skin. Most of Beowulf's comrades crept away in fear.

Only one warrior, called Wiglaf, stayed to fight alongside King Beowulf. The dragon sank its terrible fangs into Beowulf's neck. Blood was gushing out, but with Wiglaf's help Beowulf slew the dragon before he himself died.

A funeral pyre was built on a cliff top. The chieftains brought treasures, and the people built a mound over the ashes of their great king.

# Funeral for a king

The kings of East Anglia were buried at Sutton Hoo, near Ipswich. The burial site lies above a river estuary. It contains several large burial mounds.

The biggest mound was opened up in 1939. Inside it there was a long-ship big enough for 40 oarsmen. It had been used as a magnificent coffin for King Redwald, who died in 624. The wood of the ship had rotted away, but there were still marks in the soil showing where it had been.

For the burial the Saxons built a cabin in the middle of the ship. This was for the precious and useful 'grave goods' which were buried with the king. He was expected to need them in his future life.

No clear signs of the king's body or its ashes were found. They may have dissolved away over the years. Even the bone lid of a purse had dissolved away, leaving only the gold and jewels which decorated it.

▼ Saxon warriors lowered the Sutton Hoo boat into a specially dug trench. After rowing it four miles down the river from Rendlesham, where Redwald had his palace, they manhandled it to the hill-top cemetery. Redwald's body and grave goods were placed in the special cabin after the boat had been lowered.

◄ The Sutton Hoo helmet is made of iron, but other metals were used for the warlike decorations on the surface. Perhaps the protective crest was meant to represent a serpent, for it seems to end in an animal's head. The helmet is extra large. It must have been padded like a crash helmet.

**This bird of prey is one of the decorations on the Sutton Hoo shield.**

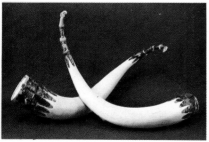

◀ The royal drinking horns. They came from the aurochs, a gigantic type of ox which is now extinct.

▶ This is the shield found at Sutton Hoo. It was made of wood and measures almost a metre from side to side. It has various metal fitments and decorations.

# Pagan beliefs

The Saxons who came to England were pagans. They all had many different gods, not just one. One of the things they did to please their gods was to make blood sacrifices. To carry out the sacrifice they killed an animal and spilled its blood in a holy place. The Saxons' holy places were forest clearings or wooden temples.

The town of Gateshead in north-east England gets its name from the Saxon words for 'goat's head'. There was probably a holy place there, where the head of a goat was left on a stake. The Saxon historian called Bede wrote about a month of sacrifice called Bloodmonth.

There were several kinds of priest of different importance. Priests slaughtered the sacrificial animals.

The letters of the pagan Saxons' alphabet were called 'runes'. They could be used to spell words in the ordinary way, but very few Saxons could read or write. The priests used runes as charms, and everyone understood their magical meaning.

Runes were linked together to make magic words. Some Saxon gold rings have been found with the magic word *erkriufltkriurithonglestepontol*. This was a spell for stopping the flow of blood from a wound.

▲ The pagan Saxons believed that people could be pestered by elves, or by dragons and demons.

▼ Warriors often had boar-crests on their helmets to make them look ferocious.

▼ Rings with runes. Runes were angular because they were often chipped onto wood or stone. They were used for spells, but our modern alphabet was introduced for books.

The pagan Saxons used magic spells. When they had heard of Christ they used his name or the sign of the cross in their magic. To cure a sick horse they cut crosses on its forehead, back and limbs, pierced its left ear and beat it with a stick.

▼ These urns were for human ashes. The Saxons probably believed that when the body was burned the dead person's soul was carried away in the smoke.

▲ This picture shows a magician called Mambres. His conjuring has brought him to the brink of hell.

The rune ↑ was used by itself as a prayer to Tiw, the god of death. Sometimes the sign ↑ was marked on the hilt of a sword. It was a plea to Tiw for the death of anyone who was struck by the sword.

The bodies of pagan Saxons were often burned to ashes when they died. The ashes were sometimes put in an urn marked with the same sign ↑. Here the sign was meant as a plea to Tiw to receive the person whose ashes were inside.

There is a story about a Saxon called Imma who was taken prisoner in battle. He was put in chains, but the chains kept falling off. The story says that he had magic letters hidden in his clothes to release him.

The pagan Saxons expected life after death to be much the same as life before death. A slave-girl was once buried alive in her mistress's grave so that she could go on serving her. A work-box was sometimes placed in a woman's grave so that she could carry on her embroidery after death. Important Saxons were buried with valuable grave goods like gold or precious stones.

▲ In woodland clearings like this animals were sacrificed and other rituals were carried out.

41

# The coming of Christianity

Celtic missionaries

Roman missionaries

Columba (563)

Iona

Aidan (635)

Derry

Donegal

Yeavering (627)

Lindisfarne

Paulinus (627–634)

Kells

NORTHUMBRIA

York

Whitby

Durrow

Paulinus (625)

MERCIA

Patrick (432)

Dunwich

Dorchester (635)

London (604)

Canterbury (602)

Rochester (604)

WESSEX

Augustine comes from Rome (597)

**KEY**

Native British church

Extent of Celtic missionary work (634–664)

◀ **Stone crosses were erected to mark places where Christians worshipped in the open air.**

**Some of the Irish monks travelled hundreds of miles, on horseback and on foot, to spread Celtic Christianity.**

**The pagan king of Kent and his wife listened to Augustine's preaching when he first arrived from Rome.**

In the year 597 a band of missionaries, led by Augustine, arrived in Kent and began a successful preaching campaign. As time went by, the pagan settlers of England were converted to Christianity.

In 625 the pagan King Edwin, who ruled the kingdoms of Deira and Bernicia, wanted to marry the Christian Kentish princess Ethelburga. Her family refused until Edwin promised that he would allow priests into his palace to help her carry on as a Christian. Her family then consented to the marriage.

Ethelburga was accompanied to Edwin's palace by Bishop Paulinus, one of the missionaries. Paulinus worked hard to convert King Edwin to Christianity. At last he succeeded. On Easter Day in 627 he baptized King Edwin in a specially built wooden church in York.

Now that he was a Christian himself, Edwin allowed Paulinus to preach to his subjects. In the grounds of the royal palace at Yeavering there was a grandstand where the audience could sit and listen. Paulinus could baptize his converts in the river.

When King Oswald came to the throne in 633 he was already a Christian, having lived with Irish monks on Iona. Oswald asked the monks to send him a missionary to replace Paulinus, who had returned to Kent. They sent him Aidan, who founded the monastery at Lindisfarne.

Aidan brought the Celtic type of Christianity, which was different from the Roman Christianity of Paulinus. It led to the founding of monasteries in northern England, which became great centres of learning.

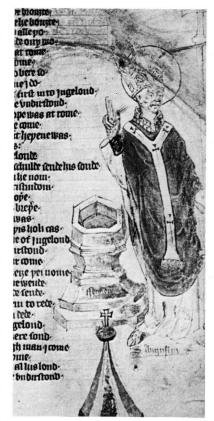

▲ This is Saint Augustine. Pope Gregory sent him on the long and dangerous journey from Rome to lead the conversion of Saxon England.

Both the Roman and the Irish missionaries converted many people in Northumbria. They baptized them in rivers.

Aidan travelled to Lindisfarne from Iona. The monasteries of Northumbria became centres for the spread of Celtic Christianity.

At Whitby, in 664, it was decided to unite Celtic Christianity with the Roman sort. Previously they had used different calendars.

# Monasteries and learning

The life and work of the monks was extremely hard. The day began at about two o'clock in the morning. The monks went straight from their beds to the monastery church for a service called matins. After that there were services every two or three hours. The monks had to wait till the afternoon for a meal. This was called *prandium*. In summer there was a meal in the evening, but in winter the monks went to bed early without another meal.

Each monastery had a number of boys who were learning to be monks. They had to get used to the hard life and the strict rules. Every afternoon the boys attended lessons in the monastery schoolroom while the monks did farm work or other labours.

There were no schools other than those of the monasteries, so reading and writing were rare skills. Books were produced in the monasteries. The monks decorated the pages of the most precious books, such as the gospels, with coloured inks. Their covers were sometimes studded with jewels. As the monasteries spread throughout England, learning and artistic skills came with them.

▶ This page of the Lindisfarne Gospels says, in Latin, 'Now the birth of Jesus Christ was like this.'

▼ Bede was the greatest Northumbrian scholar and monk. Here he is writing a book and giving it to a bishop.

**As Christianity spread, the Saxons built churches throughout England. This one still stands at Bradford-on-Avon.**

▲ This cross, made of gold and garnets, belonged to Saint Cuthbert. Cuthbert was Bishop of Lindisfarne till his death in 687.

# Alfred and the Vikings

▲ As a child Alfred stood out for his quickness in learning.

▼ In his teens Alfred fought beside his brothers.

In the year 793, Viking pirates plundered the monastery at Lindisfarne. They attacked the monastery at Jarrow in 794, and ravaged Iona in 795.

The Vikings continued these raids for over 50 years, and in 851 they started to do something worse. They began to set up permanent camps on Saxon soil. These were used as military bases, and were often on islands near the mouth of a river.

## The Vikings settle

The Vikings planned to conquer England. Sometimes they made the Saxons give them money by promising to stay away if they were paid. The Saxons called these payments *Danegeld*. After they had got their money the Vikings usually came back and conquered the Saxons.

By the start of 878 the Vikings had over-run all of England except for Wessex, which was ruled by King Alfred. Led by Guthrum, they planned to capture the king at his New Year festivities, but Alfred fled. For several days he stumbled through the icy marshes of Somerset in search of a place to set up camp. At last he came to firmer ground. He set up camp with his followers and began to call an army together. When enough men had gathered, Alfred led them against the Vikings, who quickly surrendered.

## A united England

The Vikings had come to England as pagans, but Guthrum and his leading soldiers allowed themselves to be baptized. They promised to leave Wessex and go back to eastern England and stay there. The parts which the Vikings ruled were called the *Danelaw*.

Alfred had just managed to save England for the Saxons. Later kings of Wessex began to attack the *Danelaw*. They added to Wessex bit by bit until the descendants of Alfred ruled the whole of the country. England had become one single kingdom.

In later years more Viking invaders came from Europe and conquered England. Canute, a Viking king, ruled England from 1016 to 1035.

Alfred made his people build ships. The Vikings came to England by sea. Alfred hoped that with the new ships the Vikings would be stopped.

As king he was driven into the marshes by Viking attackers. The first Vikings were Danes, but later invasions included Norwegians.

Alfred defeated the Vikings in the summer of 878. He captured Guthrum and persuaded him to become a Christian. Guthrum and 29 of his men were baptized at Aller in Somerset.

▲ Alfred laid down new laws.

▼ Alfred married his daughter to a Mercian, and this increased Alfred's influence in Mercia.

Alfred recaptured London and built up its fortifications. He also fortified the other towns that the Vikings could easily reach and attack. After securing the Saxons' territory he set about restoring prosperity.

# The Battle of Hastings

After the Battle of Hastings the Bishop of Bayeux ordered that a tapestry should be made. Its purpose was to tell the story from the Norman viewpoint. It is the largest and most famous comic strip in the world. The pictures, embroidered in woollen thread, cover 70 metres of linen cloth. It is known as the Bayeux Tapestry.

In 1042 the throne of Saxon England passed to a king called Edward. Though Edward was a Saxon he had lived in the part of France called Normandy for most of his life. He must have felt closer to the Normans than he did to the Saxons. Edward had no sons, and promised Duke William of Normandy that when he died the kingdom should pass to him.

In 1064 Edward sent Harold, Earl of Wessex, on a friendly mission to Normandy. While he was there Harold helped William to put down a rebellion. He also showed his courage by rescuing two of William's soldiers from quicksands. William knighted Harold, who in return solemnly swore to be loyal to William.

But when Edward died in 1066, Harold seized the throne of England. William set sail for England to do battle with his former ally. Harold had just fought off Norwegian invaders at a battle in northern England and he only had a weakened army to lead against William. When they met in the Battle of Hastings King Harold was killed. The leaderless Saxons fled in confusion, leaving William to take the throne of England.

# The Saxon legacy

The Saxons left behind them many things of lasting value. One of these was their language, which is the forerunner of several modern languages. The language spoken by the Saxons who lived in England developed into modern English. The language of the Saxons who stayed on the mainland of Europe developed into modern German and Dutch.

In England, many present-day boundaries were first drawn up by the Saxons. They created the English shires, or counties. Most counties and English towns have names of Saxon origin. This is because many of the towns of today have grown up from Saxon villages.

◄ The tower of Earl's Barton church, Northamptonshire, is a very good example of Saxon architecture. It is decorated with strips of stone. Other fine Saxon churches are at Bradford-on-Avon, Wiltshire, and at Jarrow in Northumberland.

## Saxon place-names

| The Saxon word | Its meaning | Its modern form | Place-name |
|---|---|---|---|
| Burh | a fortified place | burgh, brough | **Burgh Castle** (Suffolk), **Middlesbrough** |
| Ceaster, Caester | a place with an old Roman fortification | chester, caster | **Manchester, Lancaster** |
| Ford | water crossing | ford | **Stratford, Stretford** |
| Ham | a homestead | ham | **Oldham, Birmingham** |
| Ingas | tribe or kinsfolk | ing, ings | **Reading, Hastings** |
| Leah | a clearing | leigh, ley | **Leigh, Burnley** |
| Stow | a place, often religious | stow, stowe | **Stow-on-the-Wold** (Gloucestershire), **Felixstowe** |
| Ton | a homestead | ton | **Bolton** |

▼ This is known as the Alfred Jewel. Around the edge there is the Saxon inscription *Aelfred mec heht gewyrcan* which means 'Alfred had me made.' In 1693 it was found near Athelney. It seems that Alfred must have lost it while fleeing from the Danes in 878.

▲ This beautifully embroidered stole shows the prophet Jonah. It was laid in the coffin of St. Cuthbert by a Saxon king named Athelstan. Cuthbert died in 687, but because of his saintliness pilgrims came to his shrine for centuries. Athelstan made his visit in 934.

Many English surnames come from old Saxon names. The British Royal Family have a connection back to King Alfred.

Finally there are the buildings and crafts which remind us of the Saxons' great skill and wealth. A few of their churches are still in use today. Their jewellery, embroidery and beautiful books remind us of their craftsmanship. The stories and poems show us something about what they believed and how they thought.

# The story of the Saxons

## AD 410

In the third century the Saxons began to attack the North Sea coasts of the Roman Empire. England was also under attack from the Picts, who came from Scotland, and the Scots, who came from Ireland.

After the Romans withdrew, in 410, the Britons were unable to fend for them-

As the Roman empire declined, the Saxons began their piratical raids on the North Sea coasts of Europe. Then they began to settle, especially in England.

selves. They allowed Saxons to settle in eastern England. In return for this the Saxons agreed to help the Britons fight the Picts and the Scots. The Saxons then turned on the Britons, and started to conquer England for themselves.

## AD 597

England was already a patchwork of Saxon kingdoms. In 597 missionaries from Rome arrived in the kingdom of Kent to convert the Saxons to Christianity. They spread their work to the court of Edwin, king of Bernicia and Deira. The Irish were Christians already. They began missionary work

of their own in the reign of King Oswald, and many monasteries were founded. Learning flourished in the monasteries, and the monks were skilled in making beautiful books.

## AD 757

Offa was one of the most powerful kings ever to rule in Saxon England. He came to the throne of Mercia in 757. In various ways, including murder, he spread his power through the whole of England, and became the Bretwalda. Proof of his power survives today in the form of Offa's Dyke, a massive rampart and ditch about 200 kilometres long. It was built on the border between the English and Welsh peoples by some of Offa's subjects living nearby. Offa's Dyke shows that the Britons of Wales were a threat to the Saxons.

Saxon villages were soon expanding. They were centres of farming, weaving, and other industries. Some became towns, and continue as towns to the present day.

## AD 793

In this year the Vikings began to raid North Sea coasts, just as the Saxons had done. First they came for plunder. Coasts and off-shore islands were favourite sites for Saxon monasteries. These were sacked

**Christian missionaries persuaded the Saxons to give up their pagan religions. From their monasteries they spread reading and other skills throughout England.**

by the Vikings. Later the Vikings began to settle. They set up bases on islands in river mouths in England, France and Germany. From these they began to over-run large areas.

# AD 878

The final kingdom of England to be over-run by the Vikings was Alfred's Wessex. But Alfred made a very quick comeback. In the same year (878) he defeated the Vikings and made them withdraw to eastern England. He recaptured London in 886 and fought off a new wave of Viking attacks between 892 and 896.

# AD 937

Alfred's descendants gradually recon-quered land from the Vikings and ex-panded northwards. For example, in 937 King Athelstan defeated the Vikings,

Scots and Britons in the Battle of Brunan-burgh.

# AD 1016

Ethelred the Unready came to the throne of England in 978. He was forced to fight numerous battles against the Vikings. In 1013 the Viking army over-ran a large part of England, and Ethelred fled across the Channel to Normandy. In 1016 a Viking, Canute, became king of all England.

# AD 1066

With the death of Canute's son Harthaca-nute in 1042 the throne passed to Edward the Confessor, a Saxon. Since Edward had no son he promised the throne to his friend

**The Vikings who settled half of England also settled Normandy, in France. From there these Northmen, or Normans, made a final, successful attack on England in 1066.**

Duke William of Normandy. When Edward died in 1066 Harold was crowned instead of William, but William came and defeated Harold in the Battle of Hastings. William became King of England at last, and so ended the era of the Saxons.

# Famous Saxons

**Alfred the Great** (?849-899) was king of Wessex from 871 until his death. He came to the throne at a time when the Vikings were over-running the rest of England and even threatening Wessex itself. In 878 he defeated the Vikings and made peace with them. He made Wessex safer still in 886 by establishing a border line from London to Chester. Everything to the south and west of this line, including half of Mercia, the Vikings left to the Saxons. Between 892 and 896 the Vikings made further attacks, but Alfred had built strong fortifications. He had also built a strong and efficient army and navy. This time the Viking attacks failed.

As well as leading his soldiers into many battles, Alfred learned Latin. Most books were written in Latin, but Alfred wanted the best of them translated into the Saxon language. He set up a group of scholars whose job was to do this. He even did some of the work himself. He also wrote a

**Alfred deserved his title Alfred the Great. He organized and led his army, saw to the building of ships and fortifications, yet still found time for writing and prayer.**

book of wise laws to help his people live in peace. Alfred achieved all this in spite of a mysterious and terrible illness which afflicted him for most of his life.

**Bede** (674-735) became the greatest monk and scholar of his time. When he was seven years old his relatives took him to the monastery at Wearmouth. He remained there as a novice monk for about four years.

At the age of about eleven he moved with other monks to the monastery's other buildings at Jarrow. These were his home for the rest of his life. As he reached manhood Bede began the work which has made him famous. He began to write books. The most famous of all is his *History of the English Church and People*. This has a great many stories about the Saxons up to Bede's time.

**Caedmon** (7th century) spent most of his life as a farm worker. He was ashamed of the fact that he knew no songs. At parties every guest was expected to take a turn at singing. One day he fled from a feast in shame and hid in a cow shed. Here he had a vision in which someone stood by him and urged him to sing. Caedmon found himself singing a hymn in praise of God. He had made it up on the spot. He became a monk and spent the rest of his life composing religious songs.

**St Cuthbert** (?-687) became a monk in his teens. While still a young man he became the prior of his monastery. This made him the most important monk in the monastery, except for the abbot.

Cuthbert was eager to avoid an easy life, and he decided to live entirely alone. With

This stained-glass window from Norwich Cathedral shows Bede. The inscription is a reference to his greatest book *A History of the English Church and People.*

the help of other monks he built himself a hut on a rocky island. For several years he survived on what he could grow in the poor soil. In 685 King Egfrith and others came to his island and begged him to be the Bishop of Lindisfarne. Cuthbert became Bishop, but he returned to his island in 687 to die.

**Edwin** (?-632) was heir to the kingdom of Deira but was driven into hiding by Athelfrith of Bernicia. During his exile a mysterious stranger came to him, begging him to give up worshipping heathen gods and turn to Christianity. The stranger laid his hand on Edwin's head. He said that this was a sign by which Edwin would know him on a future occasion. Edwin took no notice – he was more concerned with defeating King Athelfrith. In 616 he finally defeated Athelfrith and became the king of Deira.

Ten years later Edwin survived an attempt on his life. The attacker had come from the king of Wessex, and Edwin set out on a punishing raid. Edwin promised that if he returned successful and safe he would let a Christian priest baptize him.

Edwin's expedition went well, but he put off his baptism time and again. At last the palace priest, Paulinus, could bear the delays no longer. He laid his hand on Edwin's head. Edwin realized that this was the man who had pleaded with him more than ten years before. He knew that he had delayed too long in becoming a Christian. He allowed the priest to baptize him, and Christianity quickly spread throughout his kingdom.

Edward the Confessor. This is the title by which we have come to know King Edward, who reigned from 1042-1066. It means he confessed, or truly believed, the Christian faith. He had Westminster Abbey built.

# The world the Saxons knew

Saxon lands

Trade routes

Vikings

Missionaries

One of the ways in which the Saxons found out about other countries was from voyages of exploration. Among the explorers were Ohthere, from Norway, and Wulfstan, who was probably from Wessex. Both made reports to King Alfred at his royal court.

Ohthere told of a voyage he made from his home district of Halgoland. He set out northwards and sailed along the coast for six days until he was well inside the Arctic Circle. At first he saw other ships, which belonged to whale hunters. Then for several days the seas were deserted. The land was deserted too, except for hunters, fowlers and fishermen. He then sailed eastwards for several days, and then southwards again. He saw walrus-hunting in the icy seas. He brought back some tusks as a gift to Alfred.

Wulfstan described how he sailed from Hedeby in Denmark to a land on the southern shores of the Baltic Sea. Here he found that the people had a strange custom when someone died. Instead of promptly burying the body they preserved it just where it lay. Wulfstan could not explain how they did it. The body could stay in a house for as long as six months without going rotten. During this time the dead person's relatives and friends spent his money on drinking and games.

Finally the body was burned. The day began with horse-racing. The dead man's friends divided whatever remained of his property into five or six piles of different sizes. They laid them out in line within a mile of the house, then rode to a point several miles further on. From there they raced each other back. The first pile they came to was the biggest. The fastest horseman came to it first and kept the pile. The others rode on, and a little further on the second-fastest horseman collected the second-largest pile of property. When all these prizes had been collected they burned the body on a funeral pyre.

Of course, very few Saxons sailed from England as explorers. Those who made the crossing to Europe were mainly merchants and pilgrims. After the missionaries had converted the Saxons to Christianity, some of them went abroad as missionaries themselves.

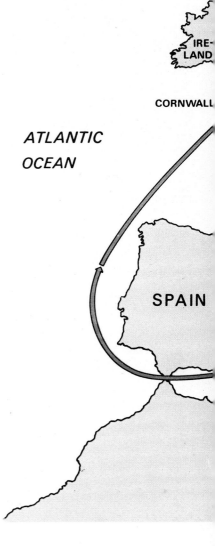

IRE-LAND

CORNWALL

ATLANTIC OCEAN

SPAIN

Ohthere's voyage, about 890 AD

HALGOLAND

Origin of
East Anglian
dynasty

NORTH
SEA

SCOTLAND
Missionaries
635 AD

VIKING
INVASIONS
793-1066
AD

Hedeby

Wulfstan's voyage, about 890 AD

European origin of Saxons

Woollen cloth

GERMANY

Wine,
pottery,
millstones

Slave boys

FRANCE

Rome

First
missionaries
597 AD

MEDITERRANEAN SEA

AFRICA

BLACK SEA

Byzantium

Fruit,
silk cloth,
silverware

Shells,
bronzeware,
spices

Alexandria

Foreign trade gave the Saxons many contacts with the rest of Europe. Slave boys were traded across the Channel and were even taken as far as Rome. Pope Gregory saw some in the market place and sent missionaries to convert the English to Christianity. Later, pilgrims from England followed the same route to Rome. Once they were Christians the English sent missionaries to Europe.

In Saxon times the Mediterranean became a dangerous place for shipping. Scarce goods still arrived from the east, perhaps by land.

# World history AD 300 to 1100

## Saxons

## Europe

## Asia

| | Saxons | Europe | Asia |
|---|---|---|---|
| **AD 300** | | | |
| | Saxons were among the peoples who were attacking Britain both before and after the Roman withdrawal of 410. By 449 they had begun the all-out conquest of the native Britons. | The Huns and other barbarians were flooding into Europe from the north and east. Constant war strained Roman resources. The Emperor Constantine (AD 306–337) ended the persecution of Christians. | The first images of Buddha were carved in China. Pilgrims began to travel to China from India along the Silk route. Roman traders established a trading post in south Vietnam. By AD 400, there was a wealthy feudal society in Japan. |
| **AD 450** | By about the year 530 most of what we now know as England was carved up among the pagan Saxons. In 597 Christian missionaries from Rome landed in Kent. They quickly converted Ethelbert, the Kentish king. | Rome was sacked by the Vandals in AD 455. Clovis, king of the Franks, became a Christian in AD 486. | The Huns invaded India and ended the time of peace and prosperity which Chandragupta II had established. |
| **AD 600** | In 627, Paulinus, one of the Roman missionaries, baptized King Edwin of Deira. Under his successor, King Oswald, an Irish monk called Aidan founded Lindisfarne Priory. The north of England soon had numerous monasteries. | The Moors, who were followers of the Moslem religion, were expanding into Europe by conquest. They were stopped in 732 by the Franks, led by Charles Martel. | The Tang dynasty ruled China from 611 to 907. During that time China enjoyed a 'Golden Age' in art. Poetry, painting and porcelain reached particularly high standards. |
| **AD 750** | The monasteries of northern England were destroyed by the Viking raids of the late eighth century. By the ninth century the only kingdom which could withstand the Viking advance was Wessex. | In 768 Charlemagne was crowned king of the Franks. He became the Holy Roman Emperor in the year 800, and later subdued the Continental Saxons. | Islamic invaders threatened northern India, but the Chola dynasty thrived in the south, and spread its cultural influence overseas. |
| **AD 900** | In 937 King Athelstan defeated Vikings, Scots and Britons in the Battle of Brunanburgh. However, by Ethelred's reign (978–1016) the Vikings were making renewed attacks, and in 1016 the throne of England passed to Canute, a Dane. | Holy Roman Empire had broken up, but was later reunited under Otto I of Germany and North Italy. Brian Boru defeated the Vikings at Clontarf, Ireland in 1020. | In China the Sung dynasty (960-1279) came to power under T'ai Tsu. Though he ruled only 13 years he made important progress in unifying the many Chinese states. |
| **AD 1050** | Edward the Confessor ruled from 1042–1066. He named Duke William of Normandy as his successor. When Harold tried to take the throne William's forces defeated and killed him in the Battle of Hastings. | El Cid, the National hero of Spain, steadily pushed back the Moors (1040–1099). Pope Gregory VII and the emperor Henry IV quarrelled over the appointment of bishops (1076). Pope Urban II preached the first crusade at Clermont. | The Sung administration was particularly efficient. Anyone wanting to be a civil servant had to pass three sets of examinations. Even then only the very best graduates were chosen. |
| **AD 1100** | | | |

| Africa | Near East | America | AD |
|---|---|---|---|
| | | | **300** |
| The site of Zimbabwe was deserted for hundreds of years. The unknown 'X-group' people of Nubia buried their dead in rich tombs. Romans closed pagan Egyptian temples in 380. Many pagan monuments were wrecked by Christian fanatics. | Emperor Constantine moved the eastern capital of Rome to Byzantium, laying the foundation of the Byzantine Empire. People made pilgrimages to Jerusalem. Tombs and buildings were carved into the rock at Petra. | The Maya people in Mexico built great temples and observatories. The Maya used their own form of hieroglyphic writing, and worked out a very accurate calendar, but they had no knowledge of the wheel, and made little use of metals. | **AD** |
| | | | **450** |
| Under the Byzantine Emperor Justinian I Belisarius captured the north of Africa in 534. It became part of the Byzantine Empire. | In Persia, the Sasanid Empire was approaching its height. Christians were persecuted and great Zoroastrian scriptures were written. | The Mexican city of Teotihuacan was flourishing at this time. It had more than 100,000 people. | **AD** |
| | | | **600** |
| The kingdom of Ghana (covering a different area from modern Ghana) was founded in the early eighth century. It drew its wealth from trade across the Sahara. | In 641 the Sasanid Empire fell to the Arabs, who imposed the Moslem religion and Arabic language. | Towards the end of this period the Toltecs created an empire in the Valley of Mexico. The Maya civilization was also thriving in Central America, and erected the standing calendar stones at Tikal. | **AD** |
| | | | **750** |
| On the Indian Ocean seaboard Moslems set up trading ports. In west Africa the Hausa people produced fine leather goods, and the Kanem-Bornu Empire was founded. | The Arabs made great discoveries in the world of medicine. Al Razi (860–935) discovered many ways of treating measles and smallpox. In mathematics, the Arabs brought the numerals 1–9 from India and introduced zero. | It had been a custom in Maya society to erect carved and inscribed stone slabs to commemorate great events. During the ninth century one centre after another ceased to erect such monuments. | **AD** |
| | | | **900** |
| The kingdom of Ghana was supreme in west Africa. It was in a position to control important trade routes. Among the most valuable of the goods which its traders handled were gold and salt. | The Byzantine Emperor Leo VI (886–912) went to war with the Bulgarians. The long campaign left the Empire's frontiers little changed, but gave control over the Balkans to the Bulgarians. | The Maya civilization continued to decline in Guatemala and Mexico, though in Yucatan it was different. The Maya towns in Yucatan prospered, developing their own style of architecture. | **AD** |
| | | | **1050** |
| The Almoravids conquered west Africa and converted many of the people to the Moslem religion. Towards 1100 the Yoruba empire was created near the mouth of the River Niger. | In 1071 the Seljuks defeated the Byzantines and the emperor was forced to ask the Pope and the rulers of western Europe for help. The crusaders conquered the Holy Land but refused to hand it over to the Byzantines. | The Miztec tribe expanded under the leadership of their chief, Eight-Deer Ocelot Claw. In Peru, the Chimu people created a coastal empire, stretching for 1000 kilometres. The city of Tula was destroyed by invading northern tribes. | **AD** |
| | | | **1100** |

# Glossary   Index

**animal interlace** a design made up of interwoven animal forms.

**archaeologist** someone who studies the past from remains in the soil.

**Bretwalda** the chief Saxon king.

**churl** a member of the lower rank of freemen.

**creel** a basket for trapping fish, crabs, etc.

*Danegeld* money the Saxons paid the Danes to leave them alone.

**embroidery** designs stitched on cloth.

**freeman** a Saxon who was not a slave.

**garnet** a red semi-precious stone used in jewellery.

**grave goods** items buried with a dead person.

**hide** an amount of land.

**jesses** straps on the legs of a hawk.

**lay** a poem or song.

**matins** a religious service.

**novice** someone who is learning to be a monk or a nun.

*prandium* the monks' main meal.

**quern** a pair of grindstones.

**retainer** a freeman who belonged to the bodyguard or household of a king.

**runes** the letters of the Saxons' original alphabet.

*scriptorium* (pl. *scriptoria*) the writing-room at a monastery.

*seax* the Saxons' traditional sword.

**thane** a member of the upper rank of freemen.

**thatch** straw or reeds used for roofing.

**warp** the threads running vertically on a loom.

**wattle and daub** a framework of wood with clay smeared on it, used to make walls, etc.

*wergild* a person's money value in Saxon law.

**Witan** the group who advised a Saxon king.

**yarn** thread used in the making of cloth.